THE ART OF WALLPAPER
Color • Draw • Create

THE ART OF WALLPAPER
Color • Draw • Create

Thames & Hudson | V&A

First published in the United States of America in 2017 by Thames & Hudson
in association with the Victoria and Albert Museum, London.

www.thamesandhudsonusa.com

ISBN 978-0-500-48020-5

Printed and bound in China by Toppan Leefung Printing Limited

V&A Publishing
Supporting the world's leading
museum of art and design,
the Victoria and Albert
Museum, London

CONTENTS

A BRIEF HISTORY OF WALLPAPER

'Whatever you have in your rooms think first of the walls …'

William Morris, 'The Lesser Arts of Life', 1882

WALLPAPER — fragile, ephemeral, easy to replace — has often disappeared from historical record. The history of wallpaper has therefore been based largely on pieces that have passed into archives and museum collections, papers that survive in historic buildings and those represented in visual records of interiors. The Victoria and Albert Museum began collecting wallpapers from its foundation in 1856 and today has one of the finest collections in the world.

Since the advent of mass-produced wallpapers in the mid-19th century, wallpaper has featured in almost every home. Although it has generally been thought of as a backdrop to interior decoration, its role in the overall decorative scheme of a room is a vital one. The choice of wallpaper affects the mood and style of a room and influences the choice of other furnishings. The pioneering Arts and Crafts designer William Morris recognized the importance of wallpaper when he advised in one of his lectures:

'Whatever you have in your rooms think first of the walls, for they are that which makes your house and home, and if you do not make some sacrifices in their favour you will find your chambers have a kind of makeshift, lodging-house look about them …'

For several centuries wallpaper was almost always designed to look like something else: tapestry, velvet, chintz, silk drapery, linen, wood, masonry or a mural. Flock-papers, imitating cut-velvet hangings, have now fallen out of fashion but were once part of the grandest and most expensive interior design schemes. Architectural papers in a variety of styles were available from the mid-18th century, and continued to be popular until the mid-19th century. As well as elaborate renderings of sculpture, architectural features, and plasterwork, there were papers printed as *trompe l'œil* imitations of masonry, marble, and later, brickwork, tiling and woodgrain. As early as 1690 Edward Butling's stock included papers in imitation of 'Wainscot' (wood-panelling) and 'Marble'. By 1795 a Parisian manufacturer, Durolin, was offering an extensive range:

'Architectural ornaments in grisaille and highlighted with gold, papers imitating Brazil wood and book spines of all sizes, grillework imitating that of bookcases, open as well as closed, trellising, brickwork, stonework, ashlar, marbles, granites, columns, pilasters, margents, banisters, cornices, architraves, statues, swags, parterres, corners, borders, panelling and overdoors of all kinds.'

Wallpapers were often perceived as an affordable substitute for more expensive materials and, as a result, were disdained as cheap imitation. In 1760 the popular French writer Madame de Genlis criticized the fashion for English wallpapers, which had driven the French Gobelin tapestries out of style:

'In the old days, when people built, they built for two or three hundred years; the house was furnished with tapestries made to last as long as the building; the trees they planted were their children's heritage; they were sacred woodlands. Today forests are felled, and children are left with debts, paper on their walls, and new houses that fall to pieces!'

Despite these debates and controversies over taste and class, the ease with which wallpaper can be produced, used and replaced has made it a durable item of home furnishing and an exciting canvas for changing fashions.

By the mid-20th century, wallpaper had become very much associated with the 'country house' look, chintzy florals and the revival of historical patterns. New and original design directions began to flower in the 1950s and 1960s, when artists and designers such as Lucienne Day revitalized the industry and initiated a trend for adventurous patterns inspired by contemporary painting, sculpture and urban environments. John Line's Palladio and Modus ranges were characterized by bold, large-scale contemporary designs, many by artists new to wallpaper.

After a period in which wallpaper fell out of fashion once again, another renaissance of sorts has been under way since the 1990s. Furnishings of the 1950s to 1970s have been rediscovered as design classics, and retro style has found a new audience and has featured in aspirational design magazines such as *Elle Decoration* and *Wallpaper**. Wallpaper can often be creatively mixed with other forms of wall decoration; a 'feature wall' papered in a bold pattern became fashionable in the 1990s, and wallpapers are now sometimes used to add interest to smaller, transitional areas such as hallways and corridors. One of the most striking aspects of contemporary wallpaper design is its rejection of traditional imagery and motifs, or the radical reworking of conventions, as seen in the translation of the pastoral landscapes of French *toile de jouy* designs into the gritty urban environments that feature in the subversive designs of Glasgow-based studio Timorous Beasties.

The following three sections of this book each focus on a key element of wallpaper design — colour, pattern and motifs — with the fourth section offering an opportunity to create entirely original patterns, using the skills developed in the previous sections. The activities are based on designs dating from the 18th century to today, which demonstrate the endless variety and creative opportunities of wallpaper design.

All the designs are from the V&A's collection and can be viewed in the galleries or study rooms of the V&A and online at www.vam.ac.uk.

1

EXPERIMENT WITH COLOUR

A huge variety of colours is found in wallpapers, and designs are often produced in many different colourways. Before the introduction of mass-manufacturing printing methods, the first wallpapers were always hand painted or stencilled. Colouring or painting wallpaper by hand is guaranteed to create an original look. Colour choices are determined by fashion and personal taste, but also the situation of a room and its use, with light colours often chosen for sunny, daytime rooms and warm tones such as yellows, pinks and reds for darker, evening spaces.

✎ *Wallpapers in their original colourways have been reproduced on the following pages, alongside the designs with all colour removed. Experiment here with colourways of your own choice.*

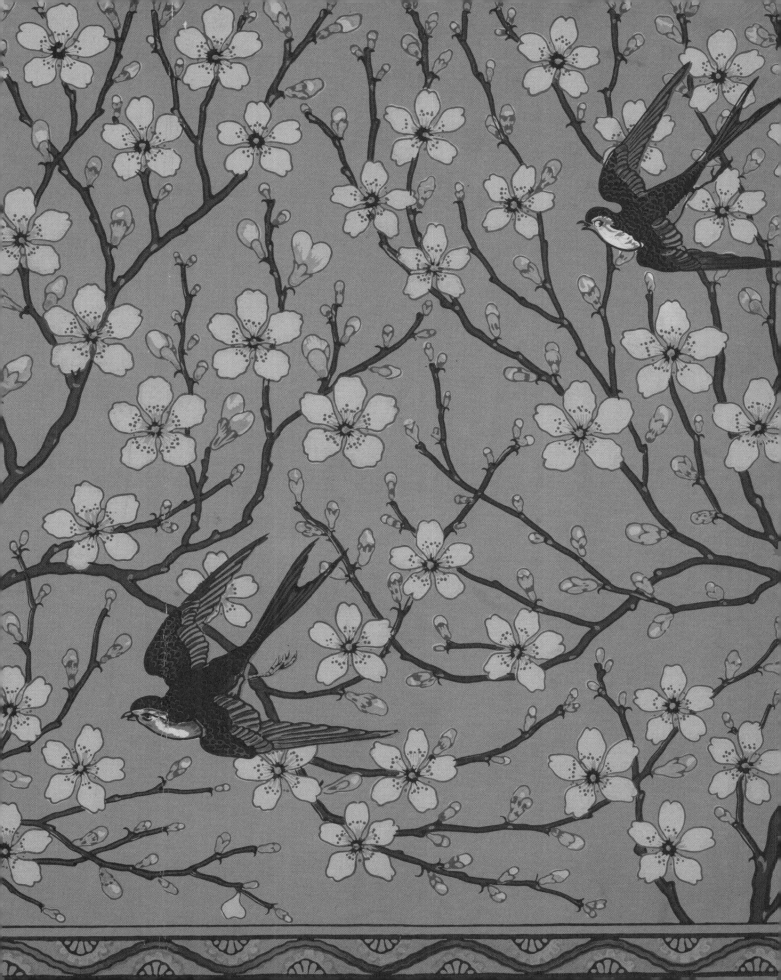

2

COMPLETE THE REPEAT

Machine-printed lengths of wallpaper first appeared in Britain in the 1840s. Repeat patterns — designed as small blocks that could be endlessly repeated in a grid — enabled the mass production of wallpaper. The best designs make a feature of the repeat and maximize its aesthetic possibilities. William Morris was an expert in combining bold lines with beautiful curving shapes and small botanical details. He advised: 'Do not be afraid of large patterns … a pattern where the structure is large and the detail much broken up is the most useful'.

✎ *Designs featuring bold repeat patterns have been reproduced on the following pages. Redraw and complete the patterns to create a continuous design. You may wish to draw grid lines, indicated at the edges of the page, to guide you.*

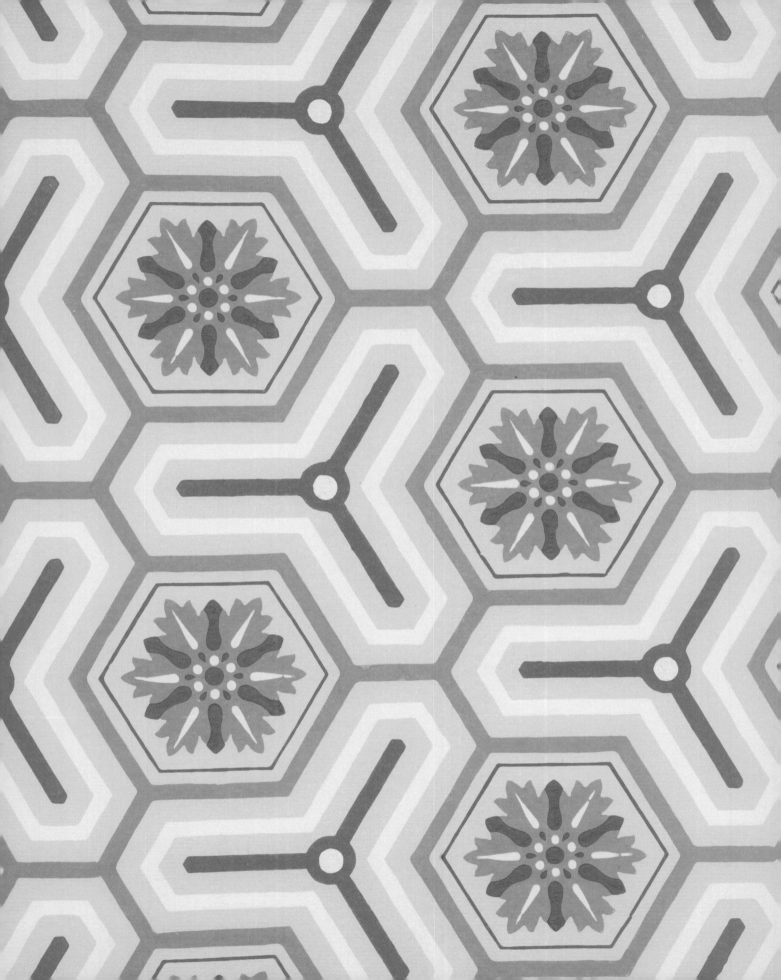

D. 745-97

№ 16.

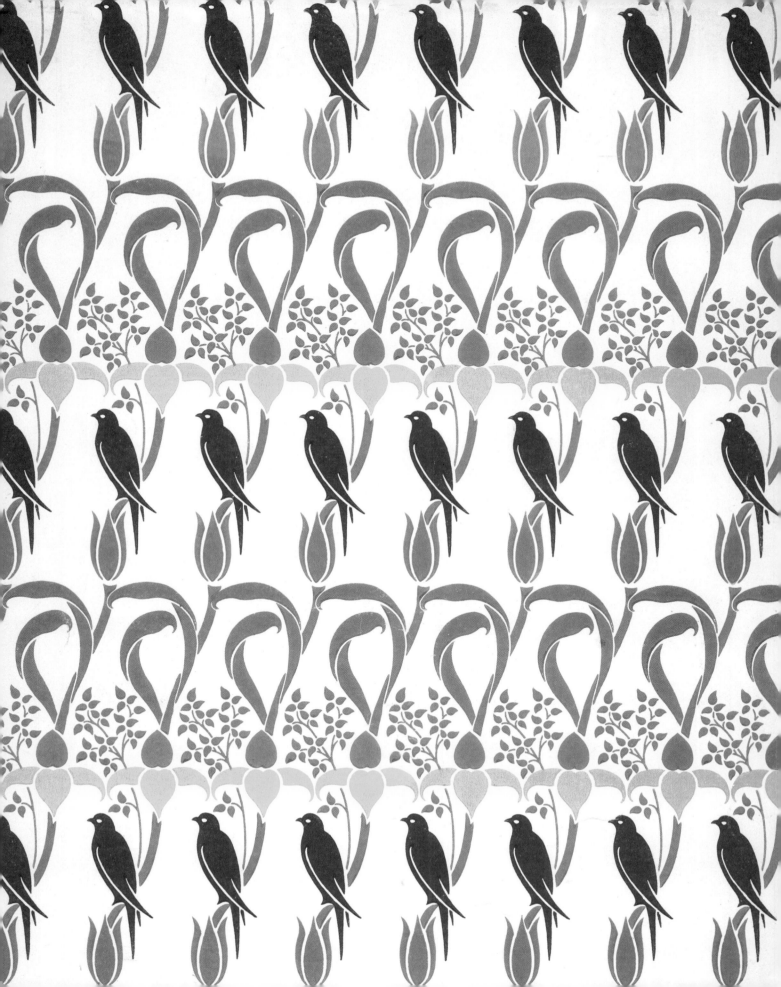

3

FILL IN
THE GAPS

Some of the earliest 17th-century painted Chinese wallpapers were prized in Europe because of the absence of a repeat pattern and the quirky, unique differences between one length of paper and another. Although repeat designs have become dominant due to manufacturing methods, hand-drawing wallpaper opens up a world of creative possibilities. Increasing the complexity of the design is another way to introduce variety, perhaps with small drawings framed by a bigger pattern, or lots of intricate, hidden details.

✎ *Individual motifs have been removed from the following wallpaper designs, leaving borders and empty spaces. Fill in the gaps with motifs of your own design, using the grid lines to help you.*

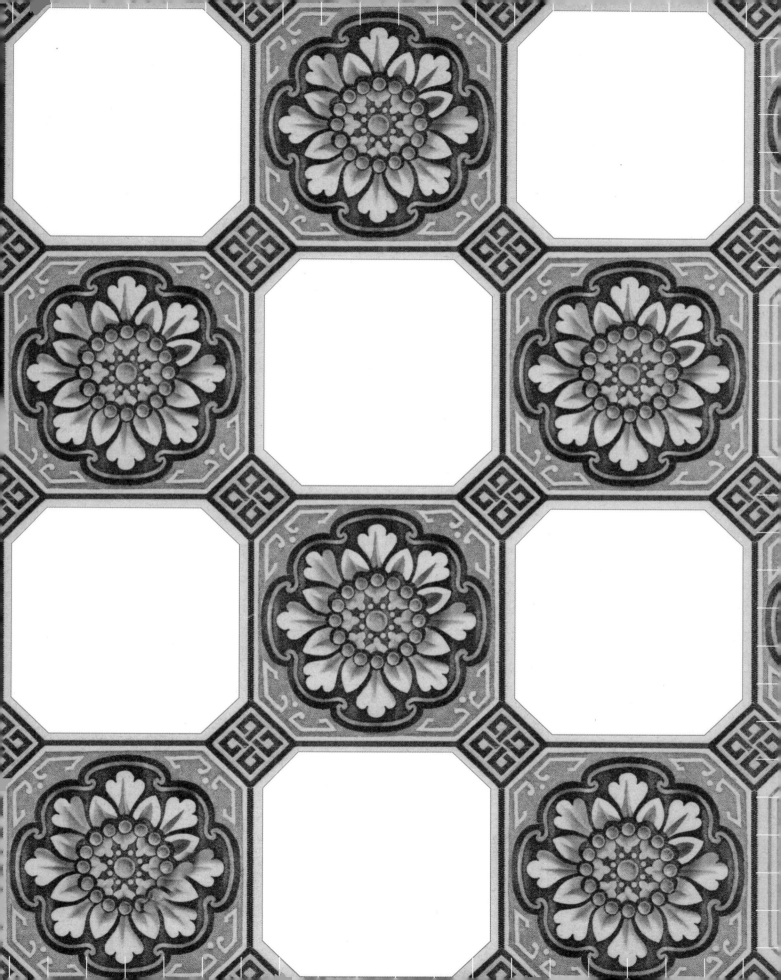

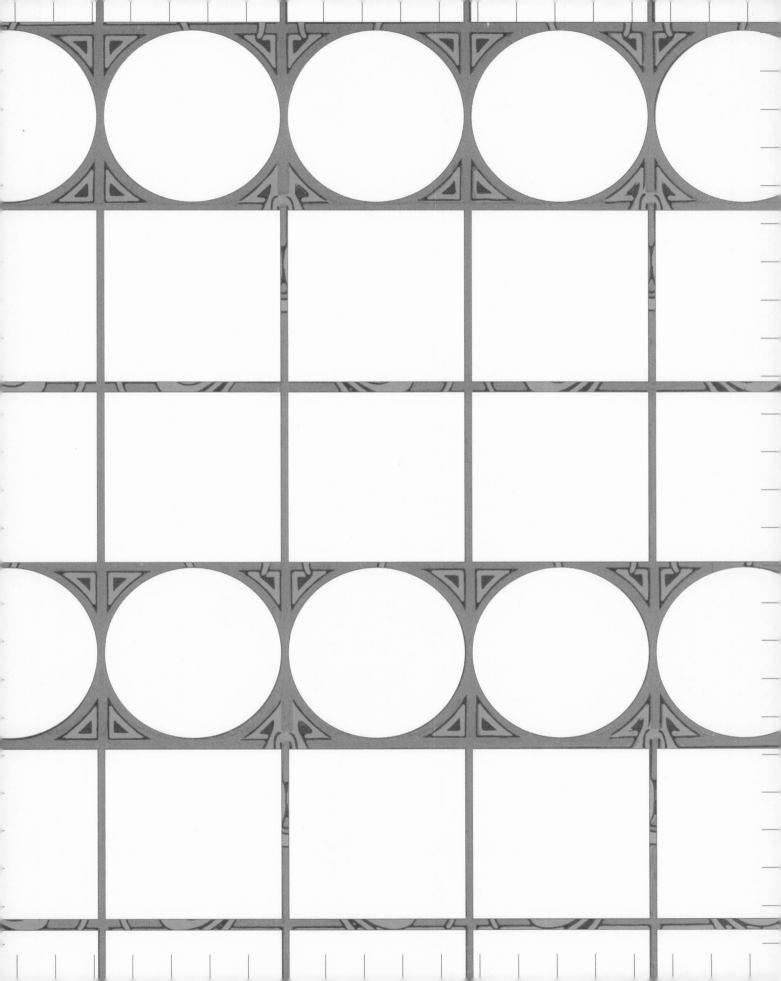

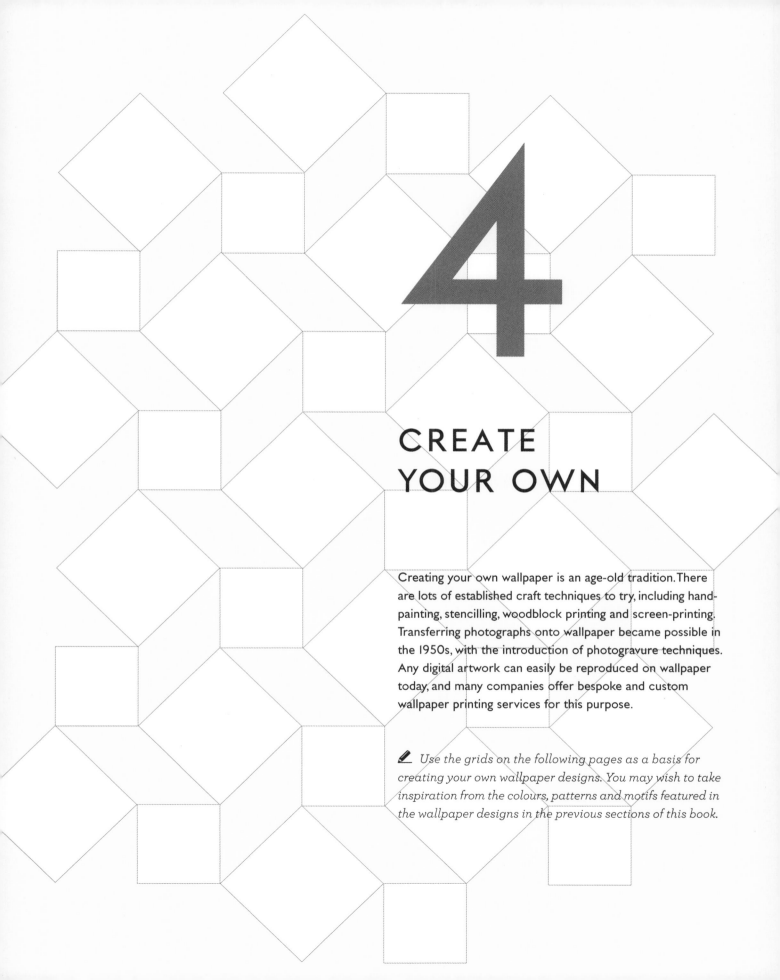

4

CREATE
YOUR OWN

Creating your own wallpaper is an age-old tradition. There are lots of established craft techniques to try, including hand-painting, stencilling, woodblock printing and screen-printing. Transferring photographs onto wallpaper became possible in the 1950s, with the introduction of photogravure techniques. Any digital artwork can easily be reproduced on wallpaper today, and many companies offer bespoke and custom wallpaper printing services for this purpose.

Use the grids on the following pages as a basis for creating your own wallpaper designs. You may wish to take inspiration from the colours, patterns and motifs featured in the wallpaper designs in the previous sections of this book.

LIST OF ILLUSTRATIONS

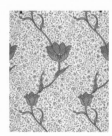

'Francesca', designed by Walter Crane,
manufactured by Jeffrey & Co.
UK, 1902
Woodblock print on paper
V&A: E.1838—1934

'Meadow Flowers', designed by
Walter Crane, manufactured
by Jeffrey & Co.
UK, 1896
Woodblock print on paper
V&A: E.5085—1919

'Corolla' from a sample book of
screen-printed wallpapers for the
architect and interior designer,
produced by Palladio Wallpapers
UK, 1955
V&A: E.444:50—1988

'Almond blossom and Swallow', designed
by Walter Crane, manufactured by
Jeffrey & Co.
UK, 1878
Woodblock print on paper
V&A: E.4037—1915

'Myrtle', designed by William
Morris (originally for needlework),
manufactured by Morris & Co.
UK, 1899
Woodblock print on paper
V&A: CIRC: 27—1954

'Fig and Peacock', designed by
Walter Crane, manufactured
by Jeffrey & Co.
UK, about 1895
Woodblock print on paper
V&A: E.1765—1914

Wallpaper designed
by Thomas William Cutler
UK, late 19th century
Woodblock on paper
V&A: E.2231—1913

'Persian', designed by John Henry Dearle
for Morris & Co., manufactured by
Arthur Sanderson & Sons Ltd
UK, about 1955
Print on paper
V&A: E.1411—1979

'Seed and Flower', designed by
Walter Crane, manufactured
by Jeffrey & Co.
UK, 1893
Woodblock print on paper
V&A: E.4033—1915

'Design for wallpaper by A. W. Pugin
UK, 1851.
Pencil and colour washes
V&A: D.699—1908

'Saxon', designed by Walter Crane,
manufactured by Jeffrey & Co.
UK, 1909
Woodblock print on paper
V&A: E.2324—1932

Design for wallpaper by Owen Jones
UK, mid-19th century
Gouache on paper
V&A: D.745—1897

Wallpaper designed by Owen Jones,
manufacturer unknown
UK, mid-19th century
Woodblock print on paper
V&A: 8341:57

Wallpaper designed by Owen Jones,
manufacturer unknown
UK, about 1858
Woodblock print on paper
V&A: 8342:41

Design for wallpaper
by Albert Hayes
UK, early 20th century
Body colour on paper
V&A: E.814—1968

'Minto', designed by C. F. A. Voysey,
manufactured by Essex & Co.
UK, 1901
Colour machine print on paper
V&A: E.311—1974

Wallpaper designed by Owen Jones,
probably manufactured by John Trumble
and Co., Jeffrey & Co., or Townsend,
Parker & Co.
UK, about 1852—74
Colour print on paper
V&A: 8337:174

'Poppy' from *Plants and their
Application to Ornament* by
Eugène Samuel Grasset, showing
designs for wallpaper, published
by Chapman & Hall
UK, 1897
Chromo-lithograph
V&A, National Art Library

Wallpaper designed by C. F. A. Voysey,
manufactured by Essex & Co.
UK, late 19th century
Colour machine print on paper
V&A: E. 315—1974

'Gourd' from *Plants and their
Application to Ornament* by
Eugène Samuel Grasset, showing
designs for wallpaper, published
by Chapman & Hall
UK, 1897
Chromo-lithograph
V&A, National Art Library

Wallpaper designed by Owen Jones, probably manufactured by John Trumble and Co., Jeffrey & Co., or Townsend, Parker & Co.
UK, about 1852—74
Colour print on paper
V&A: 8342:1

Design for wallpaper by Heussner & Co.
UK, 18th century
Pencil, ink and watercolour
V&A: 7963:59

Design for wallpaper by Lewis F. Day
UK, 1886
Watercolour and pencil on paper
V&A: E:990—1911

Design for wallpaper by Heussner & Co.
UK, 18th century
Pencil, ink and watercolour
V&A: 7963:74

Imitation tile wallpaper from a sample book produced by Cole & Son (Wallpapers) Ltd
UK, 1923—24
Colour machine print on paper
V&A: E.2651—1983

Design for wallpaper by Heussner & Co.
UK, 18th century
Pencil, ink and watercolour
V&A: 7964:19

Wallpaper, unknown designer, supplied by W. B. Simpson and Sons Ltd
UK, 1850—60
Woodblock print on paper
V&A: E.172—1934

'Quarry', designed by Lewis F. Day, manufactured by Jeffrey & Co.
UK, about 1887—90
Colour machine print on paper
V&A: E.23150—1957